Life Sentences in the Federal System

Glenn R. Schmitt, J.D., M.P.P.
Director
Office of Research and Data

Hyun J. Konfrst, M.S.
Research Associate
Office of Research and Data

Life imprisonment sentences are rare in the federal criminal justice system. Virtually all offenders convicted of a federal crime are released from prison eventually and return to society or, in the case of illegal aliens, are deported to their country of origin. Yet in fiscal year 2013 federal judges imposed a sentence of life imprisonment without parole[1] on 153 offenders. Another 168 offenders received a sentence of a specific term of years that was so long it had the practical effect of being a life sentence. Although together these offenders represent only 0.4 percent of all offenders sentenced that year, this type of sentence sets them apart from the rest of the offender population.[2] This report examines life sentences in the federal system and the offenders on whom this punishment is imposed.

There are numerous federal criminal statutes that authorize a life imprisonment sentence to be imposed as the maximum sentence.[3] The most commonly used of these statutes involve drug trafficking,[4] racketeering,[5] and firearms[6] crimes. Additionally, there are at least 45 statutes that require a life sentence to be imposed as the minimum penalty.[7] These mandatory minimum penalties generally are required in cases involving the killing of a federal official or other government employee, piracy, or repeat offenses involving drug trafficking or weapons. In fiscal year 2013, 69 of the 153 offenders who received a sentence of life imprisonment were subject to a mandatory minimum penalty requiring the court to impose that sentence.

Life Sentences Under the Guidelines System

The United States Sentencing Commission promulgates federal sentencing guidelines that provide advisory "sentencing ranges" which judges are required to consider when imposing a sentence in federal felony cases.[8] The guidelines take into account both offense behavior and offender characteristics to provide a recommended range of imprisonment, probation, or some combination of confinement and probation.

For most federal crimes there is a corresponding offense guideline specified in the *Guidelines Manual* that the Commission promulgates annually.[9] Each guideline provides one or more "base offense levels" for the offense or group of offenses referenced to it, which serves as a starting point for the determination of the guideline sentence. Most guidelines then contain additional provisions that the judge must consider in light of the offender's "real offense conduct."[10] Using these provisions, judges are required to calculate the guideline sentence that applies in each case.[11] The failure to properly calculate and consider the guidelines is reversible procedural error.[12]

To calculate the guideline sentence, the judge first determines the guideline that applies to the offense of conviction and the base offense level that applies to the facts of the case.[13] The judge then considers whether any specific offense characteristic provisions apply, along with cross references to other guidelines, and special instructions for that guideline.[14] These provisions increase or decrease the "offense level" that will determine the sentencing range in the case. The judge then applies any of the "adjustment" provisions that relate to the type of victim of the crime, the offender's role in the offense, and whether the offender obstructed justice in connection with the offense.[15] The judge also determines whether the offender has accepted responsibility for his or her crime.[16] At the conclusion of this process the judge will have determined the final offense level for the offender's crime.

Next, the judge determines a "criminal history score" for the offender, based on his or her prior criminal convictions, and places that score into one of six "criminal history categories."[17] Using the final offense level and the criminal history category, the judge consults a sentencing table[18] on which are 258 imprisonment ranges, expressed in numbers of months,[19] to find the range that corresponds to the final offense level and criminal history category that applies in the case.[20] The number of months at the high end or "top" of each range is approximately 25 percent greater than the number of months at the low end or "bottom" of that range.[21] This range of imprisonment is the "guideline range" that applies in the case.[22]

The Commission specifically provides for a life imprisonment sentence in only four of the more than 150 guidelines contained in the *Guidelines Manual*, and then only for certain acts or certain classes of offenders. These guidelines involve murder, treason, certain drug trafficking offenses, and certain firearms offenses committed by career offenders.

In first degree murder offenses, which involve the premeditated killing of another person, the guideline sentence for that offense is life imprisonment in all cases.[23] Likewise, for treason offenses, the guideline sentence is life imprisonment.[24] For certain espionage offenses,[25] and some offenses involving nuclear, biological, or chemical weapons,[26] the sentencing range associated with the base offense level[27] includes a life sentence for all offenders, although only at the top of the range.

The drug trafficking guidelines[28] specifically provide for a sentence of life imprisonment for drug trafficking offenses, but only where death or serious bodily injury resulted from the use of the drug and the defendant had been convicted previously of a drug trafficking offense. In some other drug trafficking cases, such as those involving very large quantities of drugs and where the offender has significant prior criminal history, the sentencing range can include life imprisonment, although only as the sanction at the top of the range.

The career offender guideline provides for different sentencing ranges based, in part, on the maximum penalty authorized in the statute under which the offender is convicted.[29] That guideline provides for a sentencing range that includes life imprisonment only when the offense of conviction provides for a statutory maximum punishment of life imprisonment or when the offender commits one of two specified firearms offenses[30] and the judge does not adjust the offender's sentence downward for accepting responsibility for the offense.[31]

For other offenses, although it is possible for the sentencing range under the guidelines to include life imprisonment as the top of the range, this would generally occur only in cases where multiple

Only four sentencing guidelines specifically provide for a life imprisonment sentence.

sentencing enhancements in the guidelines had applied and where the offender had a significant prior criminal record.[32]

Life Imprisonment Sentences in the Federal System

In fiscal year 2013, the courts imposed a sentence of life imprisonment in 153 cases. The number of these cases in prior years has varied, with the highest number of life sentences having been imposed in fiscal year 2009, when the courts sentenced 280 offenders to life imprisonment. As of January 2015, there were 4,436 prisoners incarcerated in the Federal Bureau of Prisons serving a life imprisonment sentence.[33] They accounted for 2.5 percent of the federal sentenced offenders in the BOP system.[34]

Number of Offenders Receiving Life Sentence
Fiscal Years 2004 – 2013

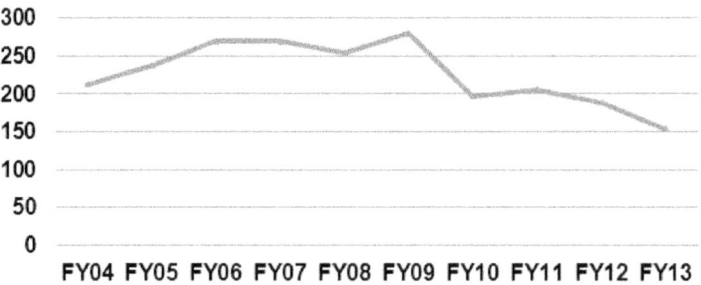

Life imprisonment sentences were imposed in a variety of types of cases in fiscal year 2013, but were most common in drug trafficking, firearms, murder, and extortion and racketeering cases. In virtually all of these cases, one or more persons died as a result of the criminal enterprise.

Offenses for Which a Life Imprisonment Sentence Was Imposed
The most common offense type for which a life imprisonment sentence was imposed in fiscal year 2013 was drug trafficking (64 cases). These cases accounted for 41.8 percent of all life imprisonment sentences that year. Even so, a life sentence is rare in drug trafficking cases, having been imposed in less than one-third of one percent of all drug trafficking cases that year.

The next most common offenses in which life imprisonment was imposed were firearms offenses (27 cases), murder (19 cases), and extortion and racketeering offenses (16 cases). Life imprisonment sentences accounted for 0.3 percent of the sentences imposed in firearms cases, 21.3 percent of the sentences imposed in murder cases, and 1.8 percent of the sentences imposed in extortion and racketeering cases.

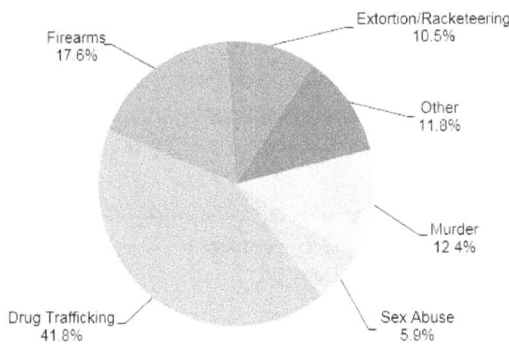

Primary Offense Type of Offenders Receiving Life Sentence Fiscal Year 2013

Life imprisonment sentences were most common in cases involving drug trafficking, firearms, murder, and extortion and racketeering crimes.

The firearms cases consisted primarily of felons in possession of a firearm[35] or the use or carrying of a firearm during and in relation to a crime of violence or drug trafficking crime, or the possession of a firearm in furtherance of those crimes.[36] All but one of the extortion and racketeering cases involved the murder, attempted murder, or kidnapping of one or more persons, often along with other violent acts, as part of the racketeering activity. The one racketeering case in which the offender was not accused of engaging in these activities involved an offender who led a drug trafficking organization and who was prosecuted under the Continuing Criminal Enterprise statute.[37]

Death or serious bodily injury also was common in the other types of cases in which a life imprisonment sentence was imposed. For example, among the robbery and auto theft cases, at least one person died in the course of each crime. In the sexual abuse and child pornography cases in this group, the offense conduct involved rape or other acts of sexual abuse, often against multiple victims who were minors.[38]

As discussed above, the sentencing guidelines call for a life imprisonment sentence in drug trafficking offenses when death or serious bodily injury resulted from the use of the drug and when the offender had one or more prior convictions for drug trafficking. But a life imprisonment sentence can also be imposed in other drug trafficking cases in which large quantities of drugs are involved, or where the court applies other sentence enhancement provisions relating to drug trafficking.[39] Crack cocaine was the drug most often involved in those drug trafficking cases in which a life imprisonment sentence was imposed. That drug was the primary drug in 34.4 percent of all life imprisonment sentence drug trafficking cases, while methamphetamine accounted for 29.7 percent and powder cocaine accounted for 21.9 percent.

**Primary Drug Type of Drug Offenders
Receiving Life Sentence
Fiscal Year 2013**

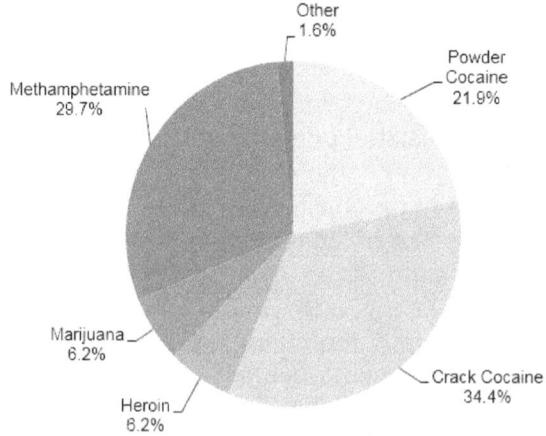

As might be expected, the quantity of drugs involved in these cases was substantial. For example, in drug trafficking cases involving powder cocaine where a life sentence was imposed, the median quantity of drug involved was more than 38,800 grams, which is approximately 86 pounds of cocaine. The table below shows the median quantities for each of the major drug types in cases where the offender was sentenced to life imprisonment.

Median Drug Quantity for Drug Offenders Receiving Life Sentence Fiscal Year 2013		
Drug Type	**Median Drug Quantity**	
	Grams	**Pounds**
Powder Cocaine	38,800	85.5
Crack Cocaine	6,338	14.0
Heroin	1,000	2.2
Marijuana	—	—
Methamphetamine	4,836	10.7

Offenders Receiving Life Imprisonment Sentences

The demographic characteristics of offenders sentenced to life imprisonment differed significantly from that of federal offenders generally. In fiscal year 2013, 45 percent of offenders receiving a life imprisonment sentence were Black, followed by White offenders (24.8%), and Hispanic offenders (24.2%). In contrast, for federal offenders generally, the racial composition was 51.5 percent Hispanic, 23.8 percent White, and 20.6 percent Black.[40]

The overwhelming majority of offenders receiving a life imprisonment sentence were men (98%). In fact, only three women were sentenced to life imprisonment that year. Among all offenders sentenced that year, 13.5 percent were women. The age of offenders sentenced to life imprisonment in fiscal year 2013 varied widely, ranging from 20 to 80 years, with an average of 37 years, only slightly higher than the average age of 36 years for all offenders in fiscal year 2013. Most life imprisonment sentences were imposed on United States citizens (133 cases). Among the 16 non-citizens sentenced to life imprisonment, six countries of origin were represented. Mexico was the most common country of origin in this subgroup of offenders (11 out of the 16 non-citizen cases).

Race of Offenders Receiving Life Sentence Fiscal Year 2013

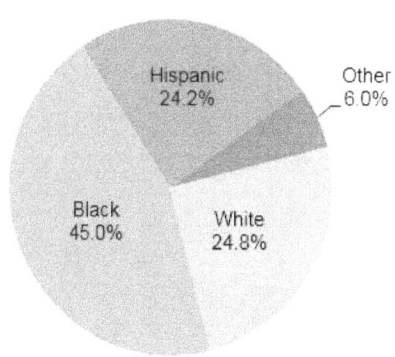

Hispanic 24.2%
Other 6.0%
Black 45.0%
White 24.8%

As might be expected, offenders sentenced to life imprisonment tended to have more serious criminal histories than federal offenders generally. Among all offenders sentenced to life imprisonment, 34.2 percent were assigned to the highest criminal history category under the sentencing guidelines, and 50 percent were assigned to one of the highest three (out of six) categories. About one quarter (24.8%) of these offenders were determined to be "career offenders."[41] Only 21.1 percent of life imprisonment offenders were assigned to the lowest criminal history category, corresponding to little or no countable criminal history.[42] In comparison, among federal offenders generally in fiscal year 2013, 22.8 percent of offenders were assigned to one of the highest three categories, with 8.5 percent assigned to the highest criminal history category, and 3.2 percent were found to be career offenders. Almost half of all offenders (46.9%) were assigned to the lowest criminal history category.

Offenders sentenced to life imprisonment were also more likely to receive an aggravating role enhancement under the guidelines than offenders receiving another punishment. This enhancement applies when the offender acted as organizer, leader, manager, or supervisor during their offense.[43] Offenders sentenced to life imprisonment received the aggravating role enhancement in one-third (33.8%) of the cases. In contrast, this enhancement applied in just 4.8 percent of all federal cases that year. No offenders sentenced to life imprisonment received a reduction in their guidelines calculation for having had a mitigating role in the offense.[44]

Finally, life sentence offenders were also far more likely to have used a weapon in connection with their offense. Almost 40 percent of the offenders receiving a life imprisonment sentence were found to have possessed a weapon in connection with the offense. These offenders were either convicted of violating 18 U.S.C. § 924(c), which makes it illegal to use or carry a firearm in connection with a crime of violence or drug trafficking crime, or to possess a firearm in furtherance of such a crime, or they received an enhanced sentence through the application of a specific offense characteristic under the drug trafficking guideline because the court found that the offender had possessed a weapon in connection with the offense.[45] In comparison, for federal offenders generally in fiscal year 2013, the rate of weapon involvement in the offense was 7.7 percent.

How the Life Imprisonment Sentence Was Determined
As discussed above, there were 69 offenders who were subject to a mandatory minimum sentence of life imprisonment in fiscal year 2013.[46] Most of these offenders were drug offenders (35 cases). The next most common offense type in which a mandatory minimum penalty applied was murder (14 cases). None of the offenders in these cases received relief from the application of the mandatory minimum penalty and, therefore, the court was required to impose the life imprisonment sentence.[47]

In the remaining 84 cases no mandatory minimum penalty applied requiring the court to impose the life imprisonment sentence; however, the recommended sentencing range under the sentencing guidelines nevertheless provided for a lengthy sentence. In fact, in more than three-quarters (79.8%) of the 84 cases, a life sentence was the only term of imprisonment provided for under the guidelines. In the remaining 17 cases, the guideline sentence was a range of imprisonment. The average minimum of the guideline range in these cases was 344 months, although the bottom of the range varied from 180 months to 420 months.[48] In most of these cases (14 cases, 82.4%) a sentence of life imprisonment was included as the top of the guideline range.[49] In fact, in only three cases (2.0%) in fiscal year 2013 did the court impose a sentence above the applicable guideline range in order to impose a life imprisonment sentence.

Of the 153 cases in which a life imprisonment sentence was imposed in fiscal year 2013, the offender was convicted after a trial in 105 cases. This represents a trial rate of 68.6 percent for these cases, a rate that is considerably higher than the three percent trial rate for all federal cases in fiscal year 2013. One factor causing this significantly higher trial rate likely was the applicability of

Only 69 of the 153 offenders who received a life imprisonment sentence were subject to a mandatory minimum penalty requiring that sentences be imposed.

statutory mandatory minimum penalties, which apply regardless of whether the offender pleads guilty or asserts his or her right to trial. A mandatory minimum penalty of life imprisonment applied in 48 of the 105 life sentence cases that went to trial. As discussed above, even in the cases where no mandatory minimum penalty applied the guideline sentencing range often was a life imprisonment sentence. If the offender was unable to obtain a favorable plea agreement with the government, the offender might believe that there was little to lose by requiring the government to prove its case against him.

De Facto Life Imprisonment Sentences

Although only a small number of federal offenders are sentenced to life imprisonment each year, there are other federal offenders sentenced to extremely long specific terms of imprisonment. In many of these cases the length of sentence imposed is so long that the sentence is, for all practical purposes, a life sentence and likely was intended to be such by the judge who imposed it. In some of these cases, a sentence of life imprisonment was not authorized under any of the statutes of conviction[50] and the court imposed consecutive sentences for multiple counts of conviction in order to achieve the lengthy period of incarceration imposed.[51]

> In fiscal year 2013, there were 168 offenders sentenced to imprisonment of 470 months or longer.

We review these "de facto" life imprisonment sentences in this section of this report. For the purposes of this analysis, a sentence length of 470 months or longer was used as a proxy to identify cases in which a de facto life sentence had been imposed.[52] In fiscal year 2013, there were 168 offenders sentenced to imprisonment for 470 months or longer. In prior years the number of such offenders ranged from 150 in fiscal year 2008 to 232 in fiscal year 2005. As of January 2015, there were 1,983 offenders in the BOP system serving a sentence of incarceration of 470 months or longer.[53] They accounted for 1.1 percent of all federal sentenced offenders.

Offenses for Which a De Facto Life Sentence was Imposed

The most common offense for which a de facto life sentence was imposed in fiscal year 2013 was firearms (76 cases), accounting for 45.2 percent of all de facto life sentence cases. The next most common offenses in in this group were child pornography (55 cases), drug trafficking (10 cases), and sex abuse (6 cases). Even so, sentences of this length were rare in those types of cases, accounting for just 2.9 percent of all child pornography sentences, 0.04 percent of drug trafficking sentences, and 1.4 percent of the sentences in sex abuse cases.

Offenders Receiving De Facto Life Sentences
As with offenders sentenced to life imprisonment, the demographic characteristics of offenders sentenced to de fact life imprisonment sentences differed substantially from that of federal offenders generally. In fiscal year 2013, 39.9 percent offenders receiving a term of imprisonment of 470 months or longer were Black, followed by White offenders (36.9%), and Hispanic offenders (17.3%). All but two of these offenders were men. The age of these offenders ranged from 20 to 68 years, with an average age of 37 years. Most of these offenders were United States citizens (89.3%).

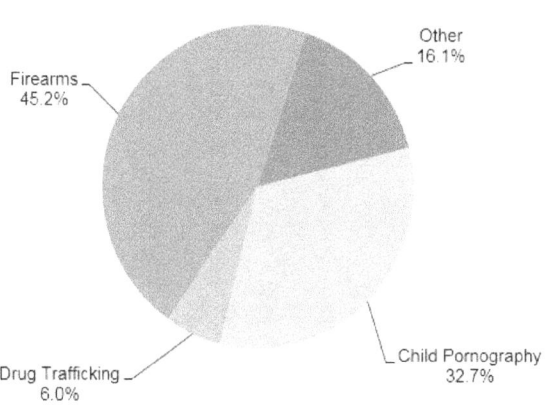

Primary Offense Type of Offenders Receiving De Facto Life Sentence Fiscal Year 2013

De facto life sentence offenders also tended to have more serious criminal histories than federal offenders generally. More than one-third (37.5%) of the de facto life imprisonment offenders were classified into one of the three highest criminal history categories, compared to only 22.8 percent of offenders generally. Career offenders accounted for 14.4 percent of this group.

The offense characteristics of offenders sentenced to de facto life sentences also were more serious than for federal offenders generally. De facto life sentence offenders also were more likely to have had an aggravating role in the offense for which they were convicted (*e.g.*, as an organizer, leader, manager, or supervisor). In about one-quarter (23.4%) of the de facto life sentence cases, the offender was found to have had this role, compared to just 4.8 percent of cases for offenders generally. In only one case did the court reduce the sentence imposed for the offender's mitigating role in the offense (*i.e.*, finding that the offender played a minor or minimal role in the offense).

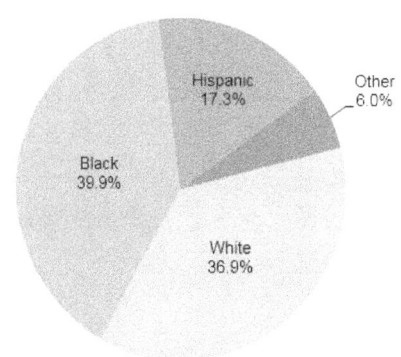

Race of Offenders Receiving De Facto Life Sentence Fiscal Year 2013

De facto life sentence offenders were also far more likely to have used a weapon in connection with their offense. Half (50.0%) of these offenders were found to have possessed a weapon in connection with their offense.

How the De Facto Life Sentence Was Determined
The average sentence imposed in these cases varied widely overall and by offense type. The sentences imposed ranged from 471 months to 3,120 months (260 years). A sentence of 100 years or longer was imposed in 22 of the 168 cases (13.1 %). The highest average sentences in this group were for child pornography cases at 832 months, followed by 820 months in sex abuse cases. In firearms cases, the average sentence was 760 months, and in drug trafficking cases the average sentence was 487 months.   Given that the average age of the offenders in this group was 37 years, these average sentence lengths support a presumption that the judges imposing them intended the offenders to remain incarcerated for the remainder of their lives in most instances.

In virtually all of the de facto life imprisonment cases a statutory mandatory minimum sentence applied, however, those minimum penalties appear to explain only part of the reason why these long sentences were imposed. For example, although a mandatory minimum penalty applied in 150 of the 168 de facto life imprisonment cases (89.3%), in only 45 of those 150 cases (30.0%) was imprisonment of 470 months or longer (the threshold sentence for inclusion of the case into this part of the report) required under the applicable statute. Of the 150 de facto life imprisonment cases in which a mandatory minimum sentence applied, in only 13 cases (8.7%) did the court impose a sentence that was at the minimum length required by statute.[54] All of the other sentences were longer than the mandatory minimum penalty. Even among the 45 cases where the mandatory minimum penalty was 470 months or longer, the courts still imposed a sentence longer than the statutory minimum in 30 of the 45 cases.

In most of the de facto life imprisonment cases, the sentencing guidelines appear to have had a strong influence on the court's decision. In 133 of the 168 de facto life imprisonment cases (79.2%) the advisory guideline range provided for a sentence of at least 470 months.[55] In half of all de facto life imprisonment cases the sentence imposed was within the guideline range determined under the sentencing guidelines. In an additional 11 cases (6.5%) the courts departed upward from the guideline range to impose an even longer sentence. The government requested a sentence below the applicable guideline range in just 14 cases (8.4%), and the court otherwise imposed a sentence below the guideline range in another 59 cases (35.1%). Among the 30 cases in which the offender was sentenced above a mandatory minimum penalty of 470 months or longer, the sentence imposed was within the guidelines range in 18 of those cases.

In 63 cases the sentencing guidelines provided for a life imprisonment sentence, however, none of the statutes of conviction authorized that punishment. In the cases where the guideline sentence was life imprisonment only, the minimum guideline sentence becomes the statutory maximum sentence.[56] In the remaining cases, where the top of the guideline range was life, the maximum guideline sentence becomes the statutory maximum punishment.[57] In virtually all of these 63 cases the courts imposed a sentence on two or more counts of conviction to run consecutively in order to achieve a sentence at or near the new guideline minimum. The resulting sentences imposed ranged from 480 months to 3,120 months (260 years).

In another 101 of de facto life imprisonment cases (60.1%) a statutory maximum term of life imprisonment was authorized, yet the court still chose to impose a sentence of a term of months rather than life imprisonment. One reason for this may have been that the sentencing guidelines often did not provide for a life sentence as part of the sentencing range. In 62 of these 101 cases, although the statutory maximum sentence was life imprisonment, the sentencing range determined under the guidelines did not include that punishment. In order to impose a sentence within the sentencing guidelines structure, a sentence of a long term of months would have to have been imposed.[58] Of course, it is also possible that the court intended to give the

> The sentencing guidelines appear to have had a strong influence on the sentence imposed in the "de facto" life imprisonment cases.

offender some chance at release. In 85 of these 101 cases the sentence imposed was between 40 years and 70 years, affording the offender some possibility of a chance for release within his or her lifetime.

One of the factors leading to the high sentencing ranges in these cases could be the high trial rate. Among the 168 de facto life sentence cases, the offender was convicted after a trial in 89 cases, which represents a trial rate of 53.0 percent, substantially higher than the overall trial rate of 3.1 percent for fiscal year 2013. The presence of a mandatory minimum penalty in virtually all of these cases likely had a significant impact on the offender's decision to take the case to trial. For example of the de facto life sentence cases in which the offender went to trial, a mandatory minimum penalty of 30 years or longer applied in almost 70 percent of them (62 cases), and a minimum penalty of 40 years or more applied in almost half of them (46.1%). Many of these offenders may have concluded that there was little risk in requiring the government to prove the case at trial.

An offender's decision to insist on a trial also has an impact on the guidelines sentence that applied. For example, among the cases that went to trial, in only two did the offender receive a reduction in the offense level under the guidelines for accepting responsibility for the crime. In general, an offender's willingness to accept responsibility for his crime can reduce his final offense level by up to three levels, which corresponds to a reduction in the guidelines sentencing range that applies in the case of roughly 30 percent.[59] Offenders who exercise their right to go to trial often are not found to have accepted responsibility for their crimes and so do not receive this reduction in the guidelines range.[60]

Other Sentences Likely to Extend to the Death of the Offender

To this point, this report has analyzed cases in which the sentencing judge imposed a sentence that the offender serve the rest of his life in prison, or imposed such a long term of imprisonment that it could be inferred that the judge intended that result. However, there is a third group of cases in which the sentences imposed also are likely to result in the offenders remaining incarcerated until they die, but which does not fit neatly into either of the first two categories. In this third group of cases, there is less reason to infer that the sentencing judge intended the term of incarceration to extend to the death of the offender. In these cases, the sentence imposed is longer than the life expectancy of the offender.

For the analysis in this part of the report, Commission staff estimated the average life expectancy for federal offenders using data from National Vital Statistics System of the Centers for Disease Control.[61] Data on gender, race, ethnicity, and age was used to determine a life expectancy for each offender. Then staff examined cases in which the sentence imposed was a specific terms of months, but less than 470 months, and compared the sentence to the life expectancy calculated for the offender in order to determine whether the offender would live to the end of the sentence.[62] It is important to note that many other factors contribute to a person's life expectancy, and so the Commission's analysis for this portion of the report should be considered as only an approximation of the issue being studied.

In fiscal year 2013, there were 291 offenders sentenced to a term of incarceration longer than their estimated life expectancy. This number compares to 297 such offenders in fiscal year 2012 and 270 offenders in fiscal year 2011.

The most common offense among these "life expectancy" offenders was child pornography. Almost one-quarter (72 offenders) of the offenders whose life expectancy is less than the length of their incarceration sentence were convicted of a child pornography offense. The other most common offenses among this group of offenders were fraud (58 offenders), drug trafficking (57 offenders), firearms (38 offenders), and extortion and racketeering (13 offenders).

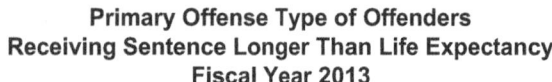

**Primary Offense Type of Offenders
Receiving Sentence Longer Than Life Expectancy
Fiscal Year 2013**

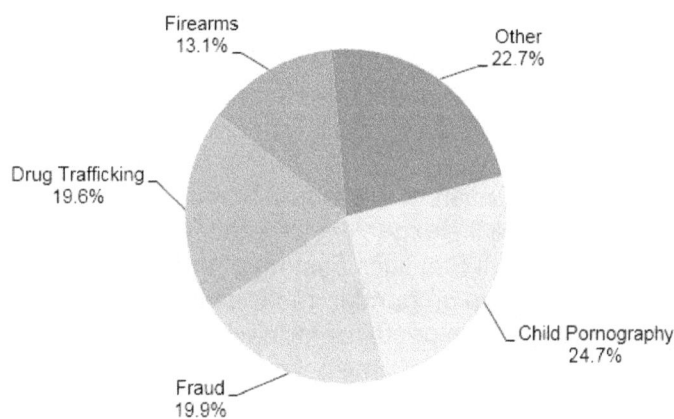

The inclusion of fraud offenders in this group sets them apart from the other two groups of life sentence offenders studied in this report, as fraud offenses generally do not involve violence. However, one aspect of the fraud cases in this life expectancy group that distinguishes them from fraud cases generally is the size of the loss amounts involved in the crime. The median loss amount in these cases (*i.e.*, in half of the cases the loss amount was higher) was more than $6 million, whereas the median loss amount in fraud cases generally in fiscal year 2013 was $195,649.

Offenders Sentenced to an Imprisonment Term Exceeding Their Life Expectancy
As might be expected, the age of the offenders in the life expectancy group is much higher than for offenders generally, or even for offenders sentenced to life imprisonment or to a de facto life sentence. The average age of the life expectancy offender

group was 66 years. More than three-quarters (80.4%) of the offenders in this group were over the age of 60, and more than one quarter (38.1%) were over the age of 70 at the time of sentencing. In comparison, the average age for all offenders sentenced in fiscal year 2013 was 36 years, and the average age for both the life imprisonment offenders and the de factor life sentence offenders was 37 years.

The race of the life expectancy offenders also differed substantially from that of the offenders in the other two groups of life sentence offenders discussed above. Among offenders sentenced to a term of imprisonment longer than their life expectancy, 65.3 percent were White, followed by Black offenders (22.3%), and Hispanic offenders (9.3%). Most of these offenders were United States citizens (94.2%).

How the Sentence Was Determined

The sentences imposed on the offenders in the life expectancy group were long, with the average sentence being 193 months. Even so, there was far more variation in the sentences imposed on the offenders in this group when compared to the de facto life sentence group, with sentences ranging from a low of two months to a high of 456 months. Despite this variation, in more than 70 percent of the cases (208 cases, 71.5%) the sentence imposed was ten years or longer and in almost 40 percent of the cases (117 cases, 40.2%) the sentence imposed was 20 years or longer.

In more than half of the life expectancy cases (148 out of 291), the offender was convicted of an offense carrying a mandatory minimum penalty. For 115 of these 148 offenders, the mandatory minimum penalty that applied in the case was 10 years or longer. Only eleven of the offenders (7.4%) convicted of an offense carrying a mandatory minimum penalty received relief from the mandatory penalty[63] by the time of sentencing.

In almost a third of these cases (91 of the 291 cases, 31.3%) a statutory maximum term of life imprisonment was authorized, however, no life imprisonment sentence was imposed on the

Race of Offenders Receiving Sentence Longer Than Life Expectancy Fiscal Year 2013

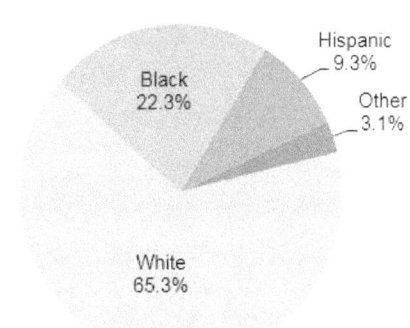

offenders in this group. Part of the reason why this was may have been because the guidelines often did not call for a life sentence to be imposed. For example, of 91 cases in which a life sentence was authorized by statute, in only seven cases was the guideline range only life imprisonment. In the remaining cases the guidelines provided for a range that included a sentence of less than life at the bottom of the range.

Even so, and as with the case of the de facto life sentences discussed above, in most of these cases the guideline sentence appears to have had substantial influence on the court's decision. For example, in three-fourths of the cases in this part of the report (216 of 291 cases, 74.2%), the minimum term of imprisonment called for under the sentencing guidelines was at least 120 months. In 111 cases (38.1%) the bottom of the guideline range was at least 240 months. In almost half of the life expectancy cases (48.8%) the sentence imposed was within the applicable guideline range and in another 4.5 percent of the cases the sentence imposed was above that range. Even among the 148 cases with a statutory minimum punishment, of the 126 cases in which the bottom of the guideline range was above the statutory minimum, the sentence imposed also was above the statutory minimum in 108 cases.

Criminal history did not appear to play any significant role in the sentences imposed on these offenders, as 57.2 percent had a criminal history score in the lowest category. Only 14.5 percent of these offenders had a criminal history score in the highest category. The trial rate in these cases also does not appear to have had a significant impact in the average sentence imposed, as almost 70 percent of these offenders (69.1%) pleaded guilty to their offense, and most of them (96.0%) received a downward adjustment to their offense level under the guidelines for accepting responsibility.[64] Of the 90 cases in this group in which the offender went to trial, in 82 cases the bottom of the applicable guideline range was at least 120 months.

Conclusion

While most federal prisoners will be released from prison eventually, a small portion of federal offenders will spend the rest of their lives there. Some of these offenders were sentenced specifically to life imprisonment, while others were sentenced to a term of imprisonment so long that the sentence will often amount to a life imprisonment sentence regardless of the age of the offender. For another small group of offenders, the age at which they committed their crime makes it unlikely that they will live to complete the sentence imposed on them. All of these offenders had committed serious crimes, and many of them had substantial criminal histories.

In most of these cases the federal sentencing guidelines called for a lengthy sentence and appear to have influenced the court to impose the sentence. In a substantial number of these cases, a mandatory minimum penalty also had an important role, either directly by requiring the sentence be imposed or by causing the advisory sentencing range determined under the sentencing guidelines to be higher than it would have been had no minimum penalty applied. While these life sentences are imposed on only a small portion of the federal offenders sentenced each year, the impact these sentences have on the lives of the offenders in those cases sets them apart from all other sentences imposed in federal cases.

Endnotes

[1] The Sentencing Reform Act of 1984 was enacted as part of the Comprehensive Crime Control Act of 1984. It abolished the use of parole in the federal system for all offenses and established a system of determinate sentencing. *See* Pub. L. No. 98-473, 98 Stat. 1987 (codified as amended in scattered sections of 18 U.S.C. and 28 U.S.C. (2012)).

[2] The average sentence imposed on all federal offenders in fiscal year 2013 was 45 months. Among those who were sentenced to a term of incarceration, the average length of imprisonment was 62 months. For information about the average sentence imposed for specific offense types, see 2013 SOURCEBOOK OF FEDERAL SENTENCING STATISTICS S-29, S-30 (2014) (hereinafter 2013 Sourcebook).

[3] *See generally* U.S. SENT. COMM'N., MANDATORY MINIMUM PENALTIES IN THE FEDERAL CRIMINAL JUSTICE SYSTEM (2011) (hereinafter Mandatory Minimum Report).

[4] The specific statutes most commonly cited in drug trafficking cases where a life imprisonment sentence was imposed were 21 U.S.C. §§ 841, 846.

[5] The specific statutes most commonly cited in racketeering cases where a life sentence was imposed were 18 U.S.C. §§ 1951, 1959, and 1962.

[6] The specific statutes most commonly cited in firearms cases in which a life sentence was imposed were 18 U.S.C. §§ 922, 924.

[7] Mandatory Minimum Report, *supra* note 3, at App. A.

[8] The sentencing guidelines also apply in Class A misdemeanor cases. U.S. SENT. COMM'N., GUIDELINES MANUAL, §1B1.9 (2014) (hereinafter USSG).

[9] *See generally* USSG App. A.

[10] See USSG Ch.1, Pt.A for a general discussion of how the guidelines were developed.

[11] *See* Gall v. United States, 552 U.S. 38, 49 (2007) (citing Rita v. United States, 551 U.S. 338, 347-48 (2007)).

[12] *Gall*, 552 U.S. at 51.

[13] See USSG §1B1.1 (Application Instructions) for a more detailed explanation of how the guidelines are to be applied.

[14] USSG §1B1.1(a)(1), (2).

[15] *Id.* at (a)(3).

[16] *Id.* at (a)(5).

[17] *See generally* USSG §4A1.1 (Criminal History Category).

[18] USSG Ch. 5, Pt.A.

[19] Six of the 258 ranges provide only for a sentence of life imprisonment. These six ranges apply in cases in which the final offense level is level 43.

[20] USSG §1B1.1(a)(7).

[21] The size of the sentencing ranges are established by statute. *See* USSG Ch.1, Pt.A (citing 28 U.S.C. § 994(b)(2)).

[22] After considering the guideline range, and whether any departures (as described in the *Guidelines Manual*) from that range are warranted, the court is also required to consider the factors listed in 18 U.S.C. § 3553(a) when imposing a sentence. USSG §1B1.1(c).

[23] USSG §2A1.1 (First Degree Murder). The sentencing guidelines do not include death as a sentence for any crime. Although the imposition of death is an authorized punishment for some federal crimes, there are separate statutory provisions providing for the consideration of that penalty in cases where the penalty is authorized. In those cases, the sentencing guidelines do not apply. *See* 18 U.S.C. § 3591.

[24] USSG §2M1.1 (Treason). The sentence applies only when the treason offense involves conduct which is "tantamount to waging war against the United States." If the conduct does not rise to that level the court is directed to determine the sentence by using a different guideline.

[25] USSG §2M3.1 (Gathering or Transmitting National Defense Information to Aid a Foreign Government).

[26] *See* USSG §2M6.1(a)(1), applying to offenses involving the use of weapons of mass destruction with the intent to injure the United States or to aid a foreign nation or foreign terrorist organization.

[27] As discussed above, once the base offense level is determined, other factors can increase or lower that level until a final offense level is determined.

[28] USSG §2D1.1 (Unlawful Manufacturing, Importing, Exporting, or Trafficking (Including Possession with Intent to Commit These Offenses); Attempt or Conspiracy).

[29] USSG §4B1.1 (Career Offender). Offenders convicted of a federal felony crime of violence or controlled substance offense are deemed to be "career offenders" if they were at least 18 years old when they committe the current offense before the court and had at least two prior felony convictions for a crime of violence or controlled substance offense. The sentencing range that applies in cases involving career offenders is the greater of the sentencing range under the guideline that applies to the current offense of conviction or the sentencing range under the career offender guideline. *Id.* at (b).

[30] Those offenses are violations of 18 U.S.C. § 924(c) or 18 U.S.C. § 929(a).

[31] *See generally* USSG §3E1.1 (Acceptance of Responsibility). The court may adjust (reduce) the offense level by two levels, and in some cases by three levels, for any offender under the guidelines if it determines that the offender has accepted responsibility for the offense. As a result, obtaining an acceptance of responsibility adjustment can have lower an offender's sentencing range by up to 30 percent.

[32] As between two offenders who commit the same offense in the same manner, the guidelines generally provide for a higher sentencing range for the offender with a higher criminal history score. *See generally* USSG Ch.4.

[33] Determined by comparing Commission sentencing records with Federal Bureau of Prisons (BOP) data on persons incarcerated as of December 27, 2014.

[34] In addition to offenders sentenced for a federal offense, the BOP also has custody of persons awaiting trial, as well as persons convicted of crimes in the District of Columbia courts and some military offenders.

[35] *See* 18 U.S.C. § 922(g) (prohibiting certain persons from shipping, transporting, possessing, or receiving a firearm or ammunition while subject to a prohibition from doing so, most commonly because of a prior conviction for a felony offense).

[36] *See* 18 U.S.C. § 924(c).

[37] *See* 21 U.S.C. § 848. In general, a continuing criminal enterprises involves a series drug crimes undertaken by a person "in concert with" five or more other persons in which the offender occupies the position of organizer, supervisor, or some other management position and obtains substantial income or resources from the criminal activities.

[38] In one case the offense conduct did not involve physical contact with a victim, but did involve interstate travel with the intent to engage in sexual acts with a person under the age of consent.

[39] USSG §2D1.1(a)(1).

[40] For additional demographic information about federal offenders see 2013 Sourcebook, *supra* note 2, at S-14 – S-19 (2014).

[41] *See* USSG §4B1.1 (Career Offender).

[42] See USSG §4A1.2 (Definitions and Instructions for Computing Criminal History) for a discussion of which offenses are counted in determining an offender's criminal history score under the sentencing guidelines.

[43] *See* USSG §3B1.1 (Aggravating Role).

[44] See USSG §3B1.2 (Mitigating Role) (offenders who play a part in the offense that makes them substantially less culpable than the average participant are entitled to a mitigating role adjustment in their guidelines calculation).

[45] *See* USSG §2D1.2(b)(1). Such a finding is made by the court, and not the jury, and can be based on a lower standard of proof than conviction under 18 U.S.C. § 924(c). The court may apply this enhancement if the weapon was present when the crime was committed. The government is not required to prove that the weapon belonged to the offender; however, the enhancement may not be applied if it was "clearly improbable that the weapon was connected with the offense." *Id*. at comment. (n.11).

[46] In a case in which the offender was subject to a statutory mandatory minimum penalty at sentencing that exceeded the applicable guideline range, the guideline sentence under the Guidelines Manual was the penalty provided by statute. *See* USSG §5G1.1.

[47] Offenders convicted of an offense carrying a mandatory minimum penalty may be sentenced without regard to that mandatory penalty if they meet one of two conditions. In cases where the offender provides "substantial assistance" to the government "in the investigation or prosecution of another" offender, the court is authorized to impose a sentence below a level established by statutes. 18 U.S.C. § 3553(e); USSG §5K1.1. Further, drug offenders who have been convicted of a drug offense carrying a mandatory minimum penalty but who meet all of the criteria of the "safety valve" provision of federal law are to be sentenced without regard to any statutory minimum sentence. 18 U.S.C. § 3553(f); USSG §5C1.2.

[48] In some of these cases another mandatory minimum penalty applied and was required to be imposed in addition to any other punishment imposed for the offense, which resulted in a minimum guideline sentence in excess of 360 months. In one other case, the court imposed a sentence of death on other counts of conviction and did not report the sentencing guideline ranges that applied to the counts of conviction on which a life sentence was imposed.

[49] Of the 258 possible sentencing ranges on the Sentencing Table used as part of the sentencing guidelines, only 21 include life imprisonment as the top of the range, and just six provide for a life sentence as the only recommended sentence.

[50] *See, e.g.*, 18 U.S.C. § 924 (providing statutory maximum penalties for firearms offenses of one, five, or ten years for most offenses); *But see* 18 U.S.C. § 924(c)(1)(B) (providing for a minimum penalty of life imprisonment

for offenses involving the discharge of a machine gun or destructive device after a prior conviction for the use or carrying of a firearm during or in relation to a crime of violence or drug trafficking crime); 18 U.S.C. § 2252 (providing statutory maximum penalties for child pornography offenses of 10, 20, or 40 years depending on the conduct).

[51] See also USSG §5G1.2 (sentencing on multiple courts of conviction).

[52] The Commission assigns a value of 470 months (39 years and two months) to sentences of life imprisonment for any statistical analysis in which a term of months is required. See U.S. SENT. COMM'N., 2013 SOURCEBOOK OF FEDERAL SENTENCING STATISTICS S-170 (2014). This sentence length is consistent with the average life expectancy of federal criminal offenders. Id.

[53] Determined by comparing Commission sentencing records with BOP data on persons incarcerated as of December 27, 2014.

[54] In two other cases the offender was convicted of a statute carrying a mandatory minimum sentence of life imprisonment, but received relief from that mandatory minimum sentence by providing substantial assistance to the government in the investigation or prosecution of another offender. See generally 18 U.S.C. § 3553(e); USSG §5K1.1. As a result, the court was authorized to impose a sentence below the statutory minimum penalty. In these two cases the court imposed a sentence above 470 months.

[55] This was because one or more mandatory minimum penalties under 18 U.S.C. 924(c) applied, requiring a mandatory penalty of more than 360 months be imposed consecutively to any other penalty imposed. When this mandatory penalty is added to the guideline sentence for the underlying (non-firearm) offense, the resulting guideline range in these cases often began at a level well above the statutory minimum penalty.

[56] USSG §5G1.1(a).

[57] Id. at (c).

[58] In many of these cases the bottom end of the guideline range was 500 months or more. This occurred because the range incorporated one or more mandatory punishments required under 18 U.S.C. § 924(c), which must be imposed consecutively to any other term of imprisonment imposed for the offense in which offender used, carried, or possessed the firearm. Section 924(c) does not specify any maximum term of imprisonment, however, most courts interpret the lack of a specified maximum punishment to imply a maximum penalty of life imprisonment. See U.S. Sent. Comm'n., Firearms Primer 9 (2014), available at http://www.ussc.gov/sites/default/files/pdf/training/primers/2014_Primer_Firearms.pdf.

[59] See generally USSG §3E1.1.

[60] For example, in fiscal year 2013, only 5.4% of the offenders who were convicted after a trial received the acceptance of responsibility reduction under USSG §3E1.1. Of the offenders who pleaded guilty, almost 98.5% received the reduction.

[61] See http://www.cdc.gov/nchs/nvss.htm.

[62] For each calculation, the Commission assumed that the offender would earn the maximum "good time" credit on their sentence. See 18 U.S.C. § 3624 (offenders sentenced to a term of imprisonment of more than one year may receive credit toward the service of their sentence "of up to 54 days at the end of each year of the prisoner's term of imprisonment," provided that "the prisoner has displayed exemplary compliance with institutional disciplinary regulations.") Under current law, a small number of offenders with a terminal illness are released each year prior to the expiration of their sentence. See 18 U.S.C. § 3582(c)(1)(A). The analysis described in this report does not account for the possibility that some offenders would be released under this provision.

[63] See supra note 47.

[64] Of course, this trial rate was still appreciably higher than the overall trial rate of 3.1 percent in fiscal year 2013. As discussed above at notes 59-60 and accompanying text, offenders who are convicted after a trial generally are not found to have accepted responsibility for their crimes and so do not receive the acceptance of responsibility adjustment to the offense level that applies in the cases under the sentencing guidelines. *See generally* USSG §3E1.1.

www.ingramcontent.com/pod-product-compliance
Lightning Source LLC
Chambersburg PA
CBHW080630180526
45168CB00007B/3112